THE TWO KINGS

THE TWO KINGS
J E S U S ✳ E L V I S

By A. J. Jacobs
Illustrated by Eric White

BANTAM BOOKS
NEW YORK   LONDON   TORONTO   SYDNEY   AUCKLAND

THE TWO KINGS
A Bantam Book/February 1994

Library of Congress Cataloging-in-Publication Data
Jacobs, A. J., 1968–
The two kings / by A. J. Jacobs ; illustrated by Eric White.
p. cm.
ISBN 0-553-37375-7
1. Presley, Elvis, 1935–1977—Humor.   I. Title.
PN6231.P695J33   1994   93-39626
818'.5402—dc20   CIP

Published simultaneously in the United States and Canada

Bantam Books are published by Bantam Books, a division of Bantam Doubleday Dell
Publishing Group, Inc. Its trademark, consisting of the words "Bantam Books" and the
portrayal of a rooster, is Registered in U.S. Patent and Trademark Office and in other
countries. Marca Registrada. Bantam Books, 1540 Broadway, New York, New York 10036.

PRINTED IN THE UNITED STATES OF AMERICA
RRC   0 9 8 7 6 5 4 3 2 1

ACKNOWLEDGMENTS

To my family, my editor Rob Weisbach, the folks at *The Nose* magazine, Gordon Kato and Elizabeth—I would buy you all Cadillacs if I could.
—A.J.

Thanks to Terri White and the whole family for love and support, A.J., Rob and Gordon for trust and extensions, Elizabeth Kairys for patience and humor, and Frank Zappa for inspiration and weirdness.
—E.W.

INTRODUCTION

On a clear night in Palm Springs in 1974, Elvis Aaron Presley confided a secret to his personal hairdresser: He believed he was Jesus Christ.

Astounding and shocking, no doubt. But what if Elvis was right?

Religious scholars and musicologists have been strangely silent on the issue. Perhaps they dismissed Elvis' claim as the ramblings of a deluded entertainer. Perhaps they were too scared to speak out. Until now.

In the interest of truth and enlightenment, an intensive three-year investigation was launched to examine the Elvis-as-Messiah theory. The research tools included the King James Bible, a stack of Elvis biographies, some ancient Christian parchments, and the soundtrack to *Blue Hawaii*.

Although dubious at first, researchers began to notice bizarre parallels and strange similarities between the King of Kings and the King of Rock 'n' Roll. Soon it became clear that Elvis may have been onto something.

Here, for the first time ever, are the results of this groundbreaking research, complete with interpretive illustrations commissioned specially for this project.

Coincidences? Perhaps. You be the judge.

Jesus walked on water. (Matthew 14:25)

Elvis surfed. (*Blue Hawaii*, 1961)

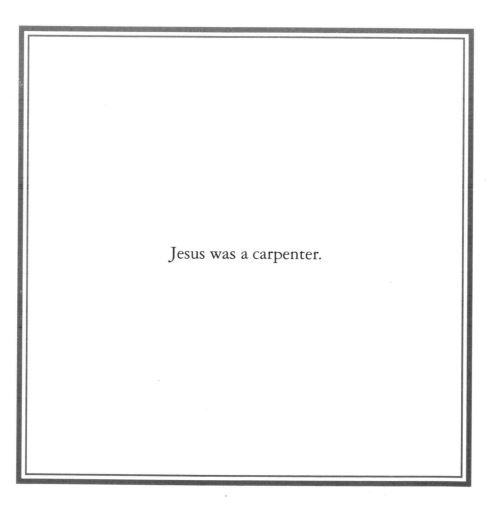

Jesus was a carpenter.

Elvis majored in woodshop.

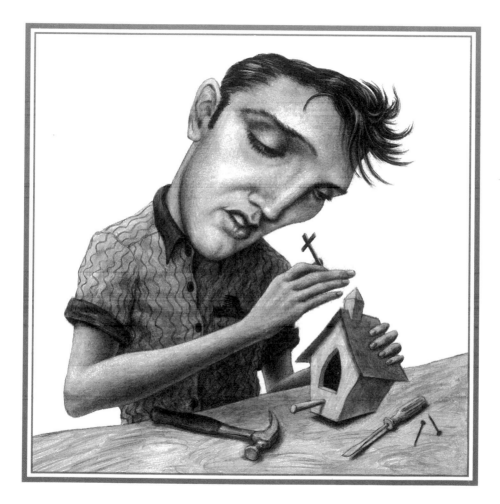

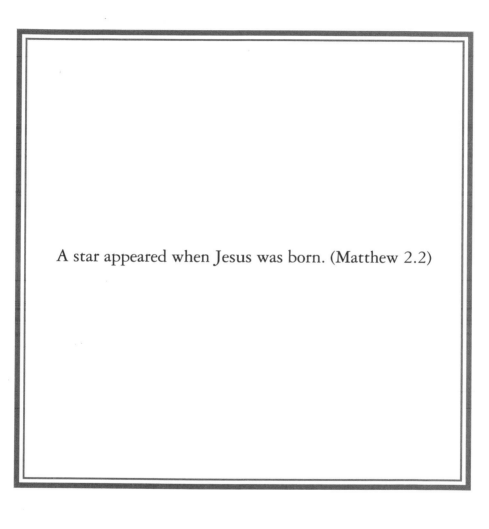

A star appeared when Jesus was born. (Matthew 2.2)

Elvis almost appeared in *A Star Is Born*.

Jesus said, "Man shall not live by bread alone."
(Matthew 4:4)

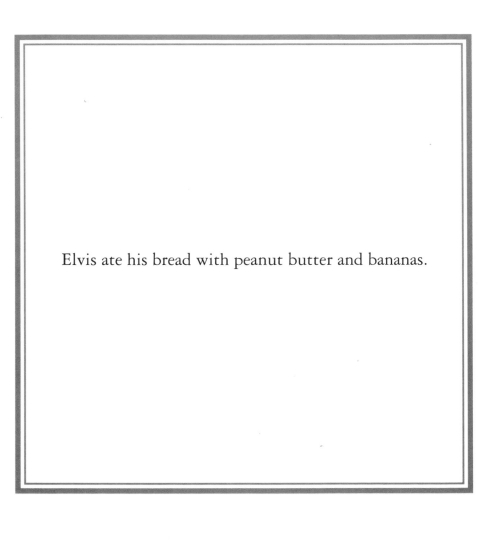

Elvis ate his bread with peanut butter and bananas.

Jesus wore the crown of thorns.

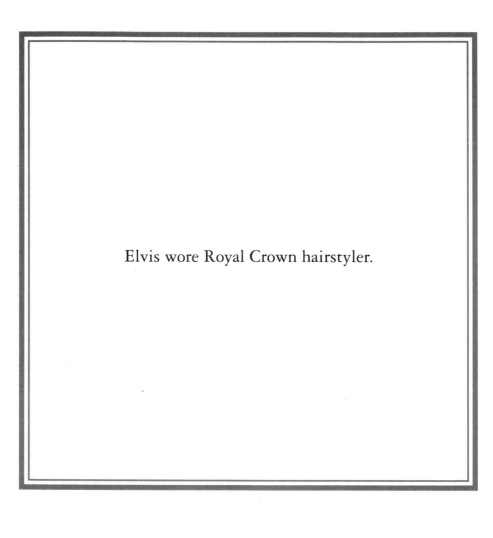

Elvis wore Royal Crown hairstyler.

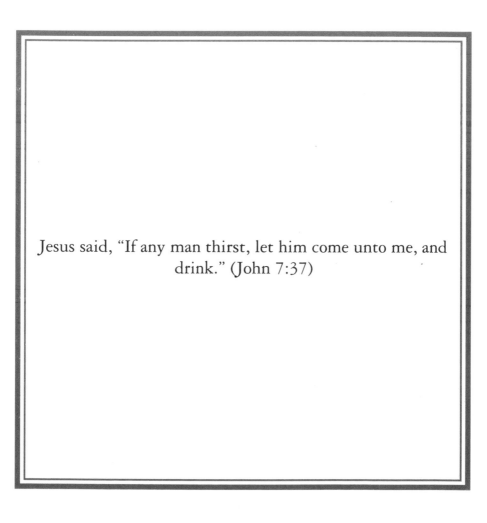

Jesus said, "If any man thirst, let him come unto me, and drink." (John 7:37)

Elvis said, "Drinks on me!" (*Jailhouse Rock*, 1957)

Jesus was Jewish.

Elvis played racquetball at the Jewish Community
Center in Memphis.

Jesus delivered us.

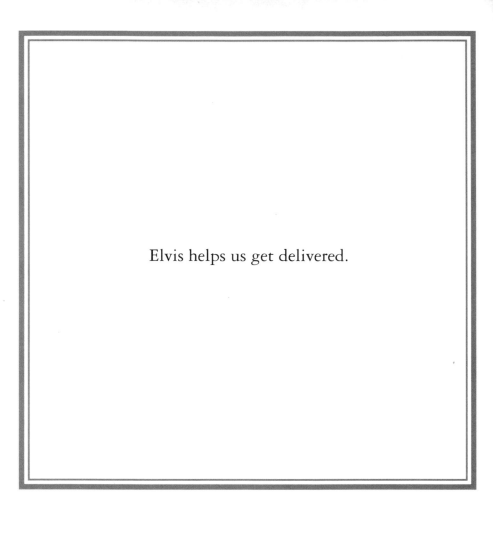

Elvis helps us get delivered.

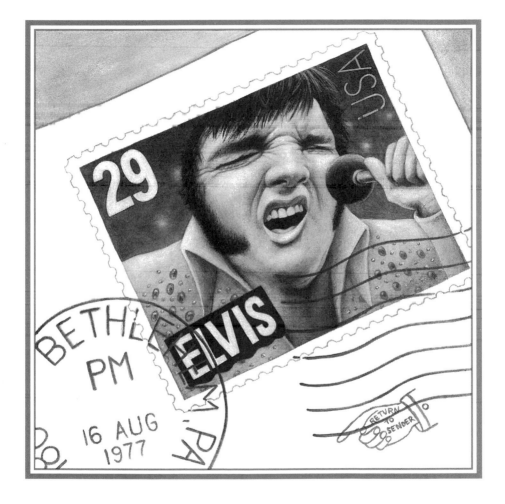

Jesus fed seafood to a hungry crowd. (The Miracle of the Loaves and Fishes, Mark 6:41)

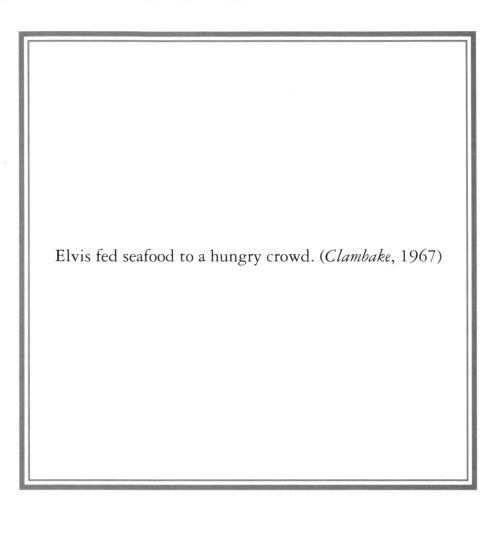

Elvis fed seafood to a hungry crowd. (*Clambake*, 1967)

Jesus is a Capricorn. (He was born on December 25th.)

Elvis is a Capricorn. (He was born on January 8th.)

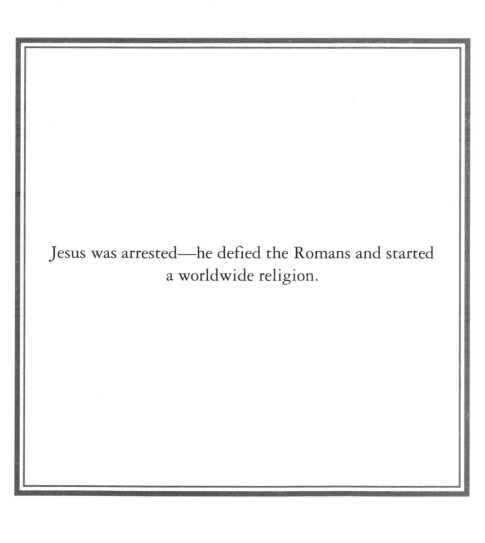

Jesus was arrested—he defied the Romans and started a worldwide religion.

Elvis was arrested—he beat up a gas station attendant.

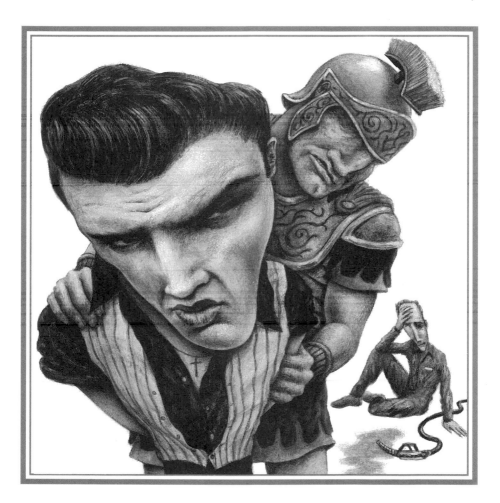

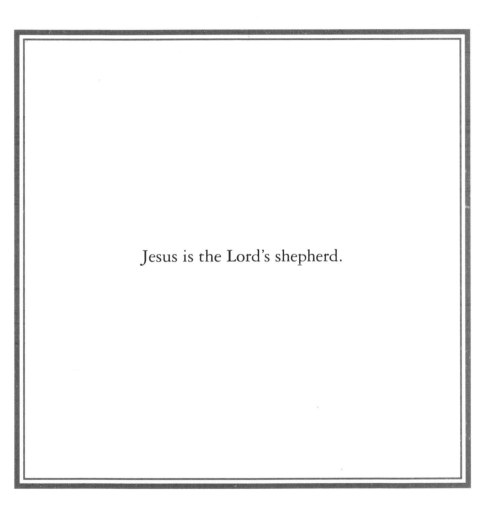

Jesus is the Lord's shepherd.

Elvis dated Cybill Shepherd.

Jesus' countenance was like lightning, and his raiment white as snow. (Matthew 28:3)

Elvis' trademarks were a lightning bolt and a snow-white jumpsuit.

Jesus said, "Many shall come in my name, saying I am Christ." (Matthew 24:5)

There are 5,000 Elvis impersonators in the
United States today.

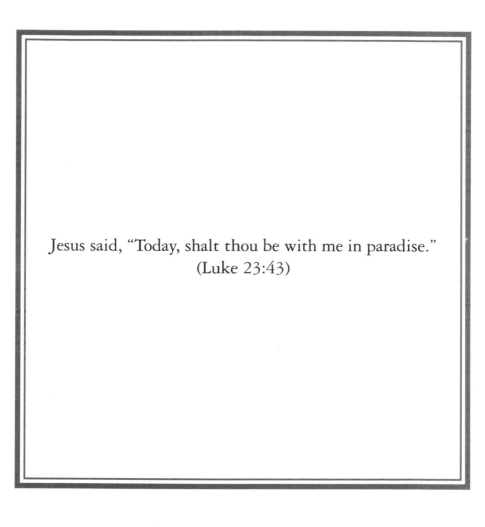

Jesus said, "Today, shalt thou be with me in paradise."
(Luke 23:43)

Elvis said, "Welcome to Paradise—Hawaiian style."
(*Paradise Hawaiian Style*, 1966)

Jesus sighting: "Afterward he appeared unto [them] as they sat at meat." (Mark 16:14)

Elvis sighting: He once appeared at a Michigan Burger King. (*The Elvis Reader*, p. 83)

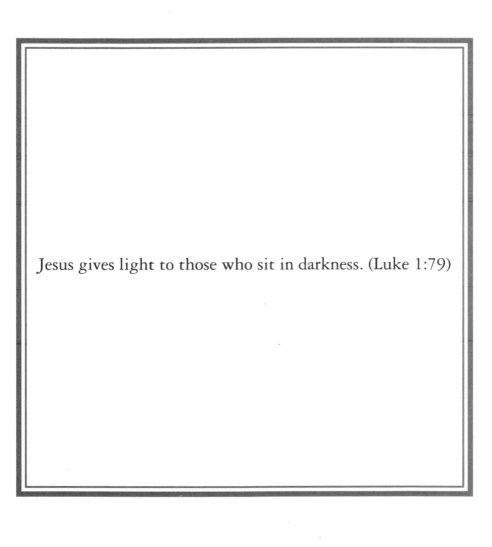

Jesus gives light to those who sit in darkness. (Luke 1:79)

Elvis studied to be an electrician. (*Elvis: His Life from A to Z*, p. 41)

Jesus is the Bread of Life. (John 6:48)

Elvis was the Toast of the Town.
(*The Ed Sullivan Show*, 1957)

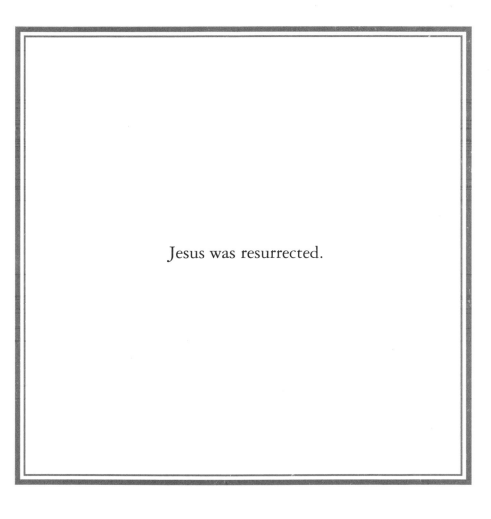

Jesus was resurrected.

Elvis had his famous comeback special in 1968.

Jesus said, "Render . . . unto Caesar the things which are Caesar's." (Matthew 22:21)

Elvis always paid his gambling debts to Caesar's Palace.

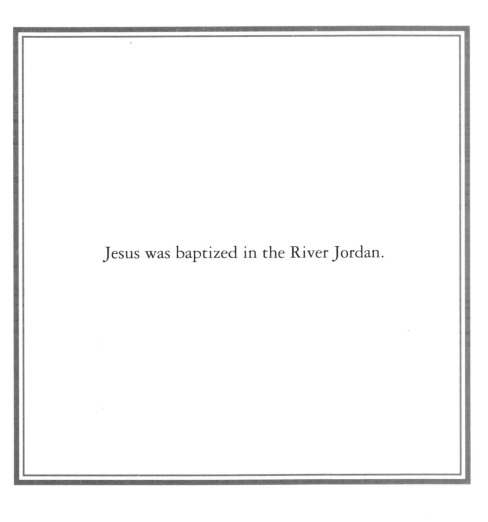

Jesus was baptized in the River Jordan.

Elvis' backup group was the Jordanaires.

Jesus is remembered on Palm Sunday in the Spring.

Elvis went to Palm Springs for the sun.

Jesus' mother was a virgin.

Elvis' mother was a virgin...at one time.

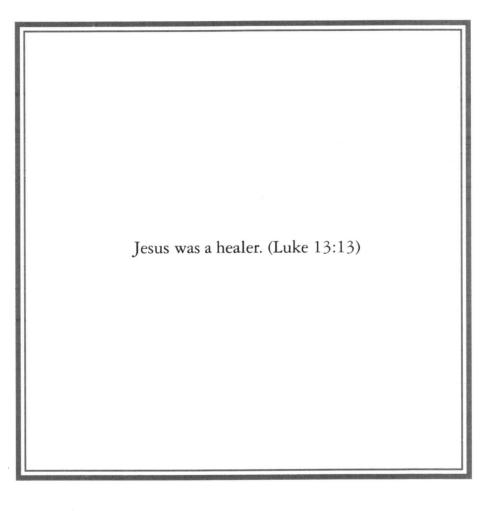

Jesus was a healer. (Luke 13:13)

Elvis passed out prescription drugs to friends and family.
(*If I Can Dream*, p. 52)

They took up stones to cast at Jesus. (John 8:59)

Elvis was often stoned.

Jesus' father gives us our daily bread.

Elvis' father had a job delivering groceries.

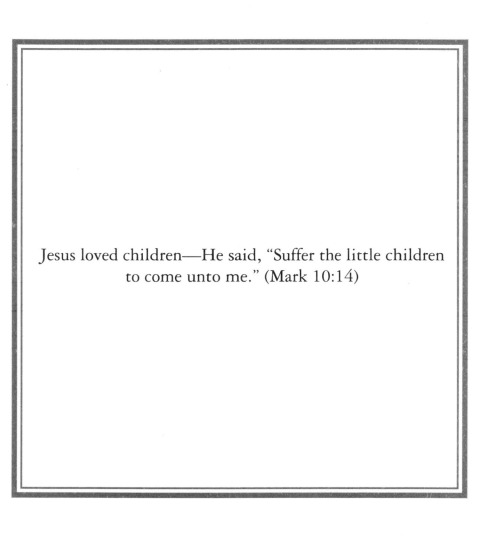

Jesus loved children—He said, "Suffer the little children to come unto me." (Mark 10:14)

Elvis loved children—he began dating Priscilla when she was fourteen. (*Elvis: His Life from A to Z,* p. 16)

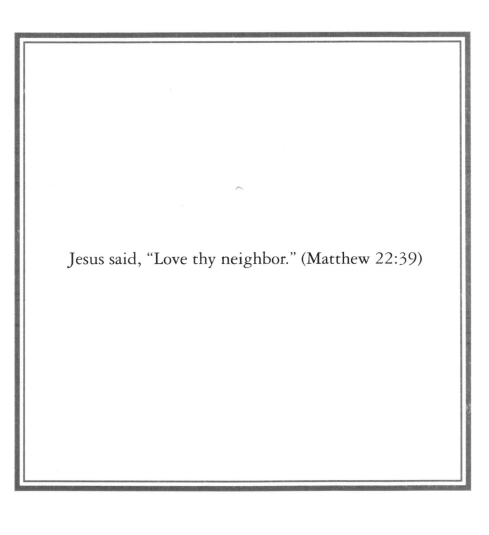

Jesus said, "Love thy neighbor." (Matthew 22:39)

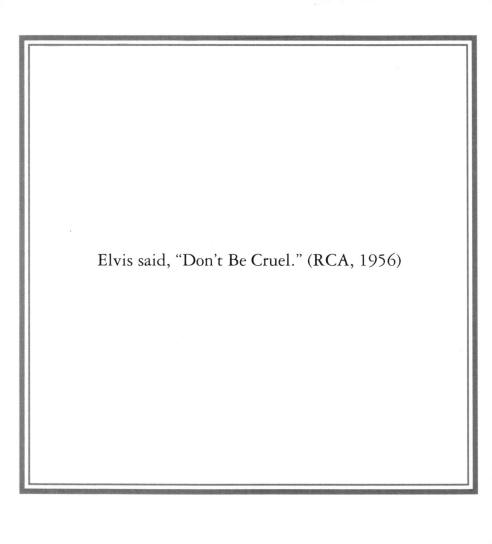

Elvis said, "Don't Be Cruel." (RCA, 1956)

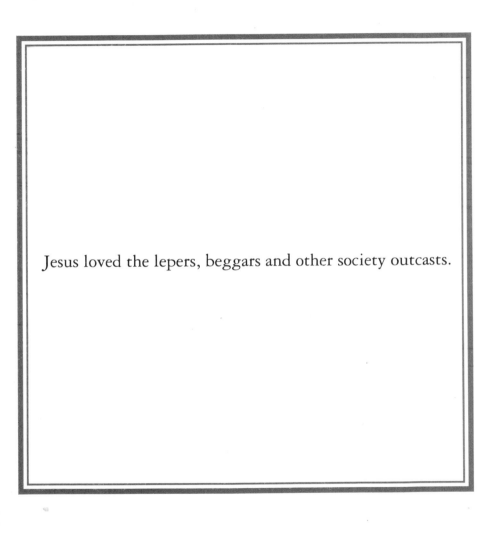

Jesus loved the lepers, beggars and other society outcasts.

Elvis loved *The Untouchables*—
he had seen almost every episode.

Jesus had irregular eating habits—he fasted for forty days and nights.

Elvis had irregular eating habits—
he liked five banana splits for breakfast.

An important woman in Jesus' life (Mary) had an
immaculate conception.

An important woman in Elvis' life (Priscilla) went to Immaculate Conception High School.

Jesus criticized the Pharisees for paying tithes without thinking. (Matthew 23:23)

Elvis took advantage of tax loopholes.
(*Is Elvis Alive?*, p. 204)

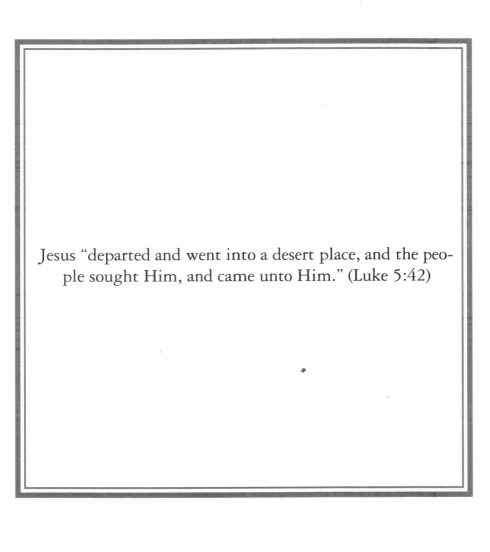

Jesus "departed and went into a desert place, and the people sought Him, and came unto Him." (Luke 5:42)

Elvis drew sellout crowds in Vegas.

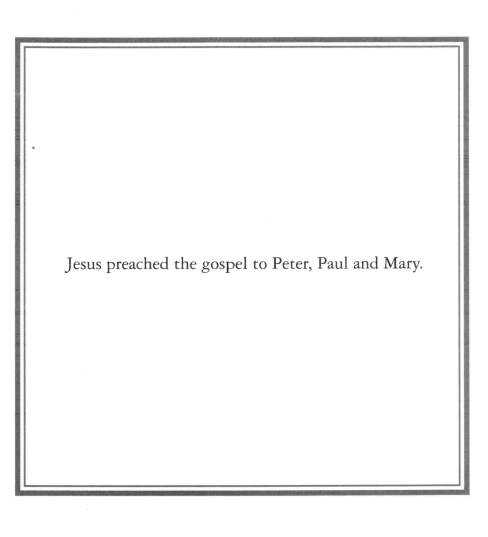

Jesus preached the gospel to Peter, Paul and Mary.

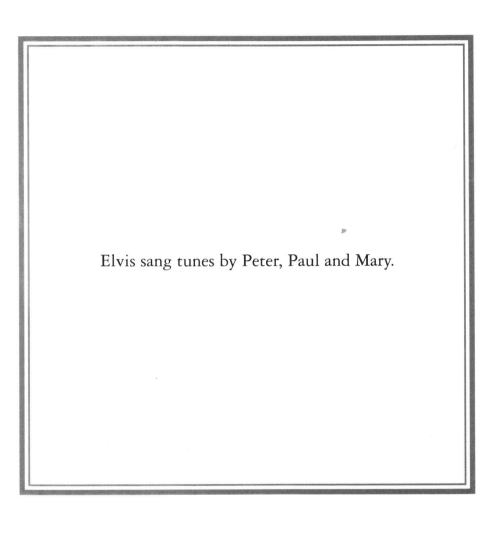

Elvis sang tunes by Peter, Paul and Mary.

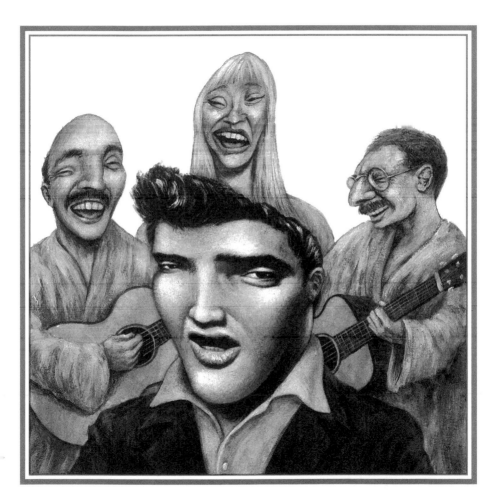

A woman touched the hem of Jesus' garment.
(Matthew 9:20)

Elvis had his clothes ripped off by screaming teenage girls.
(*E Is for Elvis,* p. 241)

Jesus' entourage, the Apostles, had twelve members.

Elvis' entourage, the Memphis Mafia, had twelve members.

Jesus took Mary Magdalene under his wing.

Elvis knew many prostitutes.

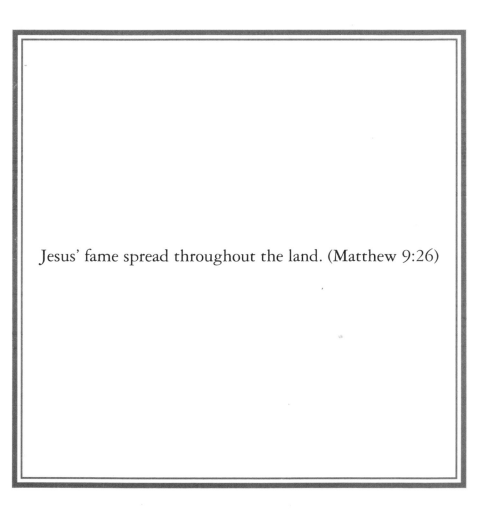

Jesus' fame spread throughout the land. (Matthew 9:26)

Elvis T-shirts are worn from New York bars to
New Guinea jungles.

Jesus said, "You will know them by their fruits."
(Matthew 7:16)

Elvis sang, "Tutti Frutti." (RCA, 1956)

Jesus was the Lamb of God.

Elvis had muttonchops.

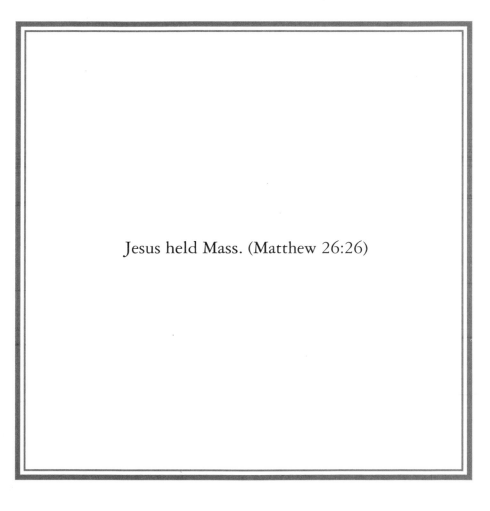

Jesus held Mass. (Matthew 26:26)

Elvis had mass—260 pounds of it.

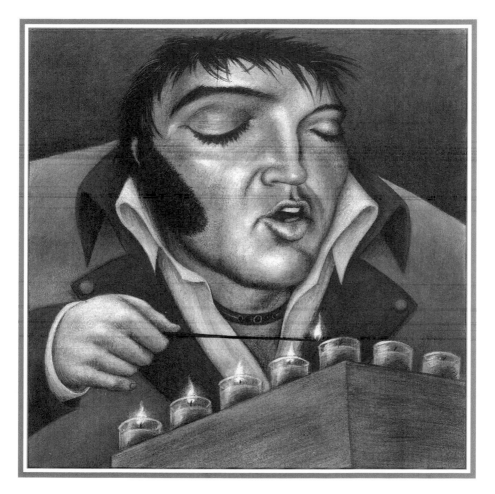

Jesus lived in a state of grace in a Near Eastern land.

Elvis lived in Graceland in a nearly eastern state.